For Colum, Irene, and Mary, who teach me every day how politics works in the smallest of societies, in hopes this will teach them something about how it works in larger ones. ~E.K.

Text ©2020 Edward Keenan
Illustrations ©2020 Julie McLaughlin

Owlkids Books acknowledges the financial support of the Canada Council for the Arts, the Ontario Arts Council, the Government of Canada through the Canada Book Fund (CBF) and the Government of Ontario through the Ontario Creates Book Initiative for our publishing activities.

Published in Canada by
Owlkids Books Inc.
1 Eglinton Avenue East
Toronto, ON M4P 3A1

Published in the United States by
Owlkids Books Inc.
1700 Fourth Street
Berkeley, CA 94710

Cataloguing data available from Library and Archives Canada

ISBN: 978-1-77147-068-1 (HC); 978-1-77147-413-9 (PB)

Library of Congress Control Number: 2015900224

Edited by John Crossingham
Design by Barb Kelly

Manufactured in Hong Kong, in September 2019, by Paramount Printing Co. Ltd.
Job #148321

C   D   E   F   G   H

ONTARIO ARTS COUNCIL
CONSEIL DES ARTS DE L'ONTARIO
an Ontario government agency
un organisme du gouvernement de l'Ontario

Canada Council
for the Arts

Conseil des Arts
du Canada

Canadä

Publisher of Chirp, Chickadee and OWL
www.owlkidsbooks.com

Owlkids Books is a division of  bayard canada

contents

The ART of the POSSIBLE

an Everyday Guide to POLITICS

EDWARD KEENAN

Art by Julie McLaughlin

Owlkids Books

Different levels

Nearly everywhere in the world, there are different levels of government that deal with different kinds of issues. Almost everyone divides the work of government up this way because, no matter where we live, we have the same kinds of problems: some of them are really small and local, and some of them are really big and affect everyone across a broad area. Big or small, these issues are all important, so the different levels of government work in coordination with each other.

National government

This is the level of government that handles issues of concern to a whole country. Often headed by a president, prime minister, or monarch, this level of government will often be concerned with things like national defence, criminal laws, and courts.

Regional government

In the United States, the regions are called states and they are headed by a governor. In Canada, they're called provinces and are headed by a premier. Other countries sometimes have different names for their regions. But regional governments all handle a large area within a country that usually has a lot of cities and towns in it. They will deal with issues for the region, often including things like education, health care, and social services, and may also deal with criminal laws.

Municipal government

Cities, towns, villages, hamlets, and other local areas are called municipalities, and they have their own governments, usually headed by a mayor. These local governments tend to deal with issues and concerns that are very close to people's homes, like garbage collection, sewage treatment, libraries, and roads.

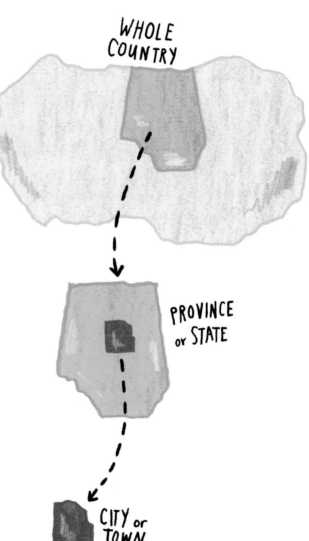

WHOLE COUNTRY

PROVINCE or STATE

CITY or TOWN

Governments are run by POLITICAL SYSTEMS

Governments need people to run them—and we need systems to choose who gets to run them and to set the rules about how they run. Across the world and throughout history, many different systems have been tried, with lots of complicated variations. But a few major options have become the most common.

 Democracy

This is a system in which people get to vote on decisions, and often vote to appoint an individual or a group of people who will have the power to make most decisions. The rulers in a democracy usually have power for a limited time only, and new leaders are chosen through elections. This is the system used in the United States, France, and South Korea, for example. We'll focus more on this system throughout the rest of the book since it's the most common one in the world today.

And it is really common. Almost all of the countries in the world today call themselves democracies, but how much power the people of those countries really have to make decisions or choose their representatives varies a lot from place to place. For instance, in some countries, elections are held, but only one party is legally allowed to run candidates. At the other extreme, some cities consider every citizen part of the government and they all get to vote on every issue, which is called direct democracy.

Today, in the United States, Canada, Germany, Brazil, and many other countries, we use a system called representative democracy. That means we elect people to look after our interests in government, and then they get to vote on all the important questions in between elections. That's the basic process of our political system.

There are really good reasons for this. For example, not everyone has the time to properly study and debate every single issue and make a smart decision about what to do. So we try to elect smart people to do that work and make those decisions for us.

A SYSTEM IN THEORY

Another system you'll sometimes hear people talk about is called anarchy. This is a system in which there is no government at all and people informally reach arrangements to govern themselves. No country in the world uses this system, but there are some activists and thinkers who suggest it as a possibility, because they think the power structure of government creates more problems than it solves. Other people often use the word *anarchy* to mean lawlessness and chaos, like in a riot or civil war.

Autocracy

This is a system in which one person has the power to make all the decisions with no restrictions. A related system is oligarchy, where a few people share the power. Autocracy and oligarchy are very similar.

One of the traditional forms of autocracy is monarchy. In what is called an absolute monarchy, someone called a king or a queen (or sometimes an emperor, prince, sultan, or some other cool title like that) is responsible for making all the decisions. The system depends on the people—the "subjects"—believing that the ruler has the right to govern and make all the decisions. As you may have learned in fairy tales and cartoons, a king or queen usually gets the job by being the son or daughter of the last monarch, which is called hereditary rule. Saudi Arabia and Eswatini are countries ruled by an absolute monarchy today.

Another form of autocracy is a dictatorship. Dictators are rulers who may give themselves any kind of title: president, chancellor, supreme leader—really, whatever they want. Dictators usually take power by using military force—by staging a revolution or a "coup" with an army. And they may use the army to control the people of their country in order to stay in power. Some dictatorships in the world today are Cuba and North Korea.

Remember how the distinction between a monarchy and a dictatorship is that usually monarchies have hereditary rule? Simple...except that plenty of monarchs are dictators, and many dictators call themselves monarchs. The honest truth is that the difference is usually in the viewpoint of who's talking: we tend to call autocrats we don't like dictators.

 Constitutional monarchy

Many countries, such as Canada, the United Kingdom, Sweden, and Japan, have a system called a constitutional monarchy. In this set up, the country is ruled by a representative democracy (often in what is called a parliament) but also has a monarch. The monarch remains politically neutral while making sure the country is run according to the rules of its own constitution, and also acts as a symbolic leader.

chapter 2

How do we decide things? And who gets to decide?

The Boston Tea Party is famous because it was one of the most important events in American history. You may have already heard of it or studied it in school because it was so important to how the United States became a country. But that's not the only reason it's interesting. If you look at it, you can learn a really good lesson about the things that are most important in politics, things that are so important that people will start a revolution over them.

The Boston Tea Party: policy vs. process

It happened way back in 1773. Even though it is called a tea party, no one was drinking from fine china cups with their pinkies in the air. It actually wasn't a party at all but a large protest. One that turned out to be the beginning of the American Revolution.

Before that, what are now the eastern U.S. states were still colonies of Britain. During the Boston Tea Party, colonists in America boarded three British ships loaded with tea being delivered to the Boston harbor. They threw all 342 chests full of dry tea leaves into the water, ruining it.

Why did they do it? They weren't against tea as a drink or anything. The reason the boat was coming to America in the first place was because the colonists enjoyed drinking tea. Instead, the colonists were protesting the Tea Act, a law passed by the British that included a tax on tea sold in the colonies in America. So it seems at first that this was a protest against a tax, right?

Not exactly.

The battle cry of the colonists throwing dehydrated drinks overboard wasn't "No tax on tea!" Instead, their slogan was "No taxation without representation."

You see, the king of Great Britain implemented laws for the colonies based on what the elected parliament in London, England, voted on. And that parliament had no colonists in it. The people living in the colonies got no vote on which taxes they paid to the king.

They weren't revolting against a tax. They were revolting against a tax that they had no say in implementing. There's a really powerful difference: they weren't just objecting to a **policy** they didn't like (the tax), they were objecting to an unfair **process** (the way that the tax was chosen).

> A **policy** is a decision that the government makes about something it will do or that people have to do. A new tax is a policy. Building bridges comes from a policy. Going to war is a policy.

> A **process** is the way a decision is made. Who gets to vote? Whose opinions are heard about the decision before it is made? Who gets the final say? The answers to these questions outline the process.

We use a process to make policies.

The truth is that the Tea Act probably would have made tea cheaper for colonists. But the colonists were angry that laws like this were being forced on them. Laws they didn't get to vote on, passed by people that they didn't get to elect. That's a problem that is much bigger than one tax. Bigger than any policy.

That's what the Boston Tea Party was about, and that's a big part of what the American Revolution was about: the colonists wanted to be involved in the process of choosing the best policies that would govern them. They were fighting for their right to decide things for themselves.

It's not just what you do, it's how you do it.

When we talk about politics or hear about it in the news, most of the discussion is about policy.

These are the kinds of things governments do. It makes sense that we spend a lot of time focusing on them.

But the most important parts of politics are not about policy at all. They're about process.

As a society, we don't just need to figure out the right things to do, we need to figure out the right way to do things.

This may be the most powerful idea in democracies. It's the idea that led to the Boston Tea Party and the American Revolution. It's an idea that is behind almost every other political revolution in history, and it's one that is involved in almost every political decision we ever make.

SHOULD TAXES BE RAISED OR LOWERED?

Should we negotiate peace with some other country or fight a war?

Should we ban plastic bags to save the environment?

Should we build a new sewer system?

A Broken Promise?

Here's an interesting thing to note: most of what politicians do once they're elected is not related to what they promised during elections. Often, people will complain about this—"Politicians never keep their promises!" they'll say, slamming their fists on the table. But it isn't even always a bad thing.

Things happen in the world that elected officials need to respond to—things no one even imagined when the election was taking place. This is normal. So the election process is mostly about deciding who we give the power to choose policies to.

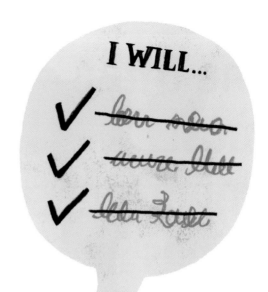

CASE STUDY

Process, Power, and Policy: The First Term of U.S. President George W. Bush

On September 11, 2001, there was a massive terrorist attack on the United States. Planes were flown into the two tallest skyscrapers in New York City (the buildings of the World Trade Center) and into the U.S. military's headquarters at the Pentagon in Washington, D.C.

What happened that day (which is now often referred to as 9/11) changed everything the American government was doing, and the actions that U.S. president George W. Bush took in the years right afterward will be remembered, for good and for bad, as very important to his country's history. He declared a "war on terrorism," and then war on Afghanistan and Iraq—countries he and his advisers claimed were affiliated with the terrorists. And he changed the laws of the United States to restrict people's freedom and to allow the government more opportunities to spy on them.

Some people think these were good things, or necessary things; other people think they were bad things. But everyone would agree that Bush did not get elected because he promised to do these things. That's because no one knew the terrorist attack was going to happen. When it did, there were no policies people had voted in favor of for Bush to implement. He had to use his power to make decisions without ever letting the people vote on them.

This is a very clear example of why it's important to remember that politics is as much about choosing who gets the power to make decisions as it is about any particular policy.

chapter 3

The three most important things in politics

Throughout modern history, Egypt was ruled by foreign countries that had conquered it in war. Then, in the 1950s, a military coup installed a dictator.

They did not hold democratic elections. People were restricted by laws and even imprisoned if they criticized the government, and police and authorities were given a lot of power. What the people wanted from their government seemed to make no difference.

But in 2011, something surprising happened.

People began to gather for a big protest in Tahrir Square in Cairo, Egypt's biggest city. Millions of people showed up to demand that the president step down. They wanted elections to choose a new government. They demanded that the government respect their civil rights.

At first, the police fought the protesters. More than eight hundred people were killed, and six thousand more were injured. But people kept on protesting, staying in the square for eighteen days. Eventually, because of the loud opposition, the president resigned. The military took temporary control of the government, promising to cancel all the restrictive laws that had made participation in politics illegal.

In 2012, the first democratic elections in Egypt's history were held. Another coup in 2013 challenged the new democratic structure, but the long-standing dictatorship had been destabilized. Now, citizens of Egypt continue to demand a voice in their political system.

This whole bit of history—the Egyptian Revolution of 2011, as it's called—can seem very different from the politics that is part of everyday life for people in Canada or the United States or other countries with long-established traditions of democracy. But it shows us some things that are true of any system in politics, anywhere in the world.

Things that matter in politics
#1 Public opinion

What people think—or public opinion—matters more than anything else in politics. Whoever is trying to govern needs the cooperation and confidence of the people they are governing. If they don't have it, their job of running the government and making decisions becomes impossible.

As the Egyptian Revolution shows (and the American Revolution we talked about in the last chapter showed, too), this is true even in systems where people don't get to vote for their government. In dictatorships or absolute monarchies, rulers still need the cooperation of the people—it's just that a lot of the time, they force people to cooperate. In many cases, they can try to keep people from questioning their authority by making debate illegal, spreading propaganda,

or imprisoning or even killing their opponents. This makes people too afraid, and often too ignorant, to try to change things.

That's really ugly and unfair. But they do it because, even in a system where one person or group of people has all the power, rulers still need to worry about public opinion. If they can't get people to cooperate, they cannot govern.

In democracies, where people elect their leaders, the importance of public opinion is even more obvious. If elected officials do things the public doesn't like, they will often lose the next election (as well as their job and power). And even if they're planning to retire from politics, they still have really good reasons to pay attention to what the public thinks and wants. Because if you're a ruler who passes laws everyone hates, people will just ignore them—the police cannot reasonably arrest everyone, so laws that most people ignore become useless. And on top of that, whoever comes along next is likely to just change all the rules you made to ones people like better.

What's right or wrong is not always the biggest factor in making political decisions. Instead, the biggest factor is public opinion—political leaders are motivated by what is popular. That is, they want people to like the things they do. And if they can't get people to like their decisions, they need people to at least accept them.

CAN PEOPLE REALLY IGNORE LAWS?

I said that people can ignore laws they don't agree with, which makes them useless. But don't they get caught and punished? Sometimes they do, but if enough people are breaking the law, it becomes impractical for police to catch them all. For example, right now in North America, many (possibly even most) people ignore highway speed limits, going faster than the posted speed almost all the time. Police catch the odd person and issue a ticket, but there are just too many cars going fast for all of them to get caught. If authorities wanted to pull over every speeder, they'd need thousands of extra police cars for every stretch of highway, and traffic would grind to a complete halt. So instead they catch only a very few people, and going a little bit faster than the speed limit is considered completely normal. Which means that the laws are very ineffective at stopping people from speeding—if you were on the highway watching most days, you would think the laws didn't exist at all.

#2 Most of it is about trying to convince people of things

During election campaigns, this is really obvious. That's when politicians are trying to convince people of one simple thing: "Vote for Me!"

But even between elections, the efforts at persuasion don't stop. There are debates and discussions about proposals that you can see on the news or online every day. People write opinion columns in the newspapers to support or oppose policies the government is considering. Citizens come out to public meetings to hear arguments and to speak about their own ideas. They phone and write letters to politicians, or organize big protests. Organized groups of activists and businesses spend a lot of money on advertising and marketing—just to convince people to support their views. And, of course, politicians and governments spend a lot of time talking about how and why people should support the things they're doing, too.

All of this debate and these attempts to convince people of things take place because public opinion is so important.

And that leads us to the third most important thing in politics.

#3 It works best when the public is informed, interested, and active

Let's look at what the most important thing about politics really means: your opinion matters, because politicians and governments will only do the things they believe most people will like.

What the second most important thing means is that people will be trying to convince you of things to make sure that your opinion agrees with theirs.

Both of these things are true even if you're not paying attention. Even if you don't care. Whether you want to or not, you are helping to shape the political process. It's just that if you ignore politics, you're making it easier for the other people—the ones who do care—to do whatever they want. And make no mistake, there are people who care, some for good reasons, some for selfish reasons.

The thing is, if you aren't paying close attention, you can be fooled pretty easily. You might wind up cooperating with things that are bad for you, or bad for society as a whole. Politics works better if all of the people are interested and educated.

That's why political activists say that "active citizenship" is a key to democracy. Active citizens are not just voters, or taxpayers, or residents. They're people who pay attention and take the time to tell their friends what they think. They tell their elected officials what they think, too.

Active citizens might read the news, attend public meetings, make phone calls, or spread their ideas on social media. They can even talk to reporters to make sure the things they care about make it onto the news. Though they aren't officially part of the government, they realize that everyone is a politician, so they make sure they are good ones. Because when public opinion is the most important thing, the members of the public who get informed, and then help inform other people, have a huge influence on how it all works. Those are active citizens.

Now that you've learned these three most important things about politics, it's time to start thinking about how public opinion is shaped—how we convince each other of things. That's what we'll talk about in the next chapter.

CASE STUDY

Active Citizenship: Jane Jacobs

In city politics in North America, Jane Jacobs is famous for being one of the most influential people in history. She was never elected to any office—she never even ran for any office—but she changed how some of the biggest cities in Canada and the United States were built.

When she lived in New York in the 1950s and 1960s, Jacobs was a writer and mother who got very upset about the way the city government was destroying neighborhoods to build highways. She organized a protest against the construction of a major highway called the Lower Manhattan Expressway through the downtown neighborhood where she lived. After years of writing about it and working with her neighbors to oppose it, the highway plan was canceled.

Jacobs then moved to Toronto. Once again, she found the city government there planning to destroy the neighborhood she lived in to build a highway, this one called the Spadina Expressway. She and her neighbors organized opposition to it, and again, after years of debate, managed to get the highway canceled. This led to the city government canceling other highways that were part of their plan.

Even though she had no formal education in city planning, she wrote books—including her most famous one, *The Death and Life of Great American Cities*—about how she

thought cities worked, and why she thought a lot of experts were building cities the wrong way. One of her biggest ideas was that neighborhoods should be built for people to walk around in rather than drive cars through. Such ideas were embraced by city planners around the world. Soon, they became the main way that experts thought about building cities. *American Scholar* magazine says she wrote "the 20th century's most influential book about cities."

And Jacobs did all that without ever getting any official power from anyone to make political decisions. She was just an active citizen who worked hard to shape her world, and succeeded.

By the way...even though Jacobs changed the minds of many experts, politicians haven't always listened to those experts. Many cities have continued to build suburbs that are made for driving, not walking, when there is no political will to do otherwise. That's another lesson about politics: you need to do more than change the experts' opinions, you need to change public opinion.

How to make a strong argument

Imagine there's something you want. Something you can't have unless a government passes a law to allow it.

For example, maybe you have a dog that needs exercise, but dogs are not allowed to run around without their leashes at your local park. Luckily, you realize that, as an active citizen, you don't have to wait around for someone powerful to decide a dog park is needed. You can do something to make this happen!

Maybe you could write a letter to your local political representative asking if an off-leash area can be set up at your park. You could suggest that one area of the park have a fence put around it so dogs can run around inside, and have some signs posted saying it's an official off-leash area for dogs.

If you want to see your suggestions implemented, you'll need to convince your government representative and your neighbors that this is a good idea. Maybe some people won't like the idea— because they don't like dogs, or because they like having the whole park to use for picnics and other things. As almost always happens in politics, there will be a debate about what is the best thing to do. But you also know that the most important thing for you to do is help make sure public opinion is on your side. You need to convince people. So what you're looking to do is make a great argument for why your dog park is a great idea.

To do that, it helps to understand how arguments and debates work. Rhetoric is a field of study about just that. Even though rhetoric can get complex, we can summarize its basic points pretty quickly.

Rhetoric 101: The three major kinds of arguments

The ancient philosopher Aristotle defined three major kinds of arguments. Let's go through them one at a time and see how they might work for you in your dog-park plan.

 Using Authority "You can trust me"

The first way to argue is on the basis of authority, or credibility. (Aristotle called this "ethos," the Greek word for "character.") This is where speakers try to convince the audience to trust them about a subject because they

- are super-experts
- have important experience that makes them credible
- are simply trustworthy people

You see politicians using this technique when they talk about their "character," like what an honest or hardworking or intelligent person they are, or when they list all the important jobs they've had and impressive things they've done. This argument boils down to this: "You should believe me because I'm a good person who knows what I'm talking about."

So, back to your dog park: you might talk about how you've been around dogs since you were very little and know a lot about taking care of them. You might mention that you volunteered in a veterinarian's office, where you learned more about what keeps dogs healthy and happy. And you could also talk about how you go to that park every day and care so much about all the people who use it.

You could also mention how you came up with another idea to build a vegetable garden that has been implemented in your schoolyard, so you have a history of coming up with good solutions to problems.

All of these arguments are more about you than about your off-leash area idea, but when people hear them, they are getting the impression that you know what you're talking about and they should trust your ideas about this subject.

Empathy: Understanding the emotions that are experienced by someone else. Feeling empathy for someone—understanding what they are going through and how that makes them feel—can often lead to sympathy, which is a feeling of being with someone, or compassion.

② Using Emotions "Look into your heart"

The second major kind of argument is emotional. (Aristotle called this "pathos," the Greek word for "suffering" or "experience.") This is where speakers try to make people passionate about a subject, and convince them to feel a certain way so that they will draw a certain conclusion.

Sometimes—for instance, when politicians want to introduce harsher criminal laws—speakers might want their audience to feel afraid. On the other hand, when politicians want to introduce more generous welfare payments, they might want to make their audience feel **empathy** for how tough life is for poor people.

Emotional arguments focus mainly on telling stories that stir up your feelings. Whatever issue the person is talking about, the gist of this argument can usually be summed up as "You should believe me because it feels right."

So, when talking about the dog park, you might tell people about how you came to know your dog when she was a few days old—a story that might remind people of their love for their own pets. You could talk about how happy she was as a little puppy, jumping and running around the backyard. And how happy that made you feel. Then you could talk about how your dog doesn't get that feeling now that she's too big for the backyard and never gets to run around.

You could talk about the painful illnesses that could result for your dog if she doesn't get enough exercise, and how sad that would make you feel.

And you could also talk about how, even without a fenced off-leash area, some people with dogs will let their pets run around without leashes on—and you could suggest that those dogs could scare or bite small children using the park, which makes people afraid.

All of these arguments use people's feelings to suggest that if they care about dogs—even if they care about people who might be scared or hurt by dogs with irresponsible owners—they should support an off-leash area.

③ Using Logic "Elementary, my dear Watson"

The third kind of argument relies on facts and evidence. (Aristotle called it "logos," the Greek word for "reason.") This is where speakers try to make an intellectual argument suggesting that the proposal they support is best when you consider the question logically. Simply put, they are saying that their suggestion is the one that is most likely to work.

For this reason, politicians will often outline the statistics to show what's causing a problem, the budget restraints they face in trying to solve it, and then explain why their solution is the one that makes more sense than the other options. This argument usually amounts to "You should believe me because the evidence shows I'm making sense."

So you could talk about the number of dog owners living in the area around the park, and how often they visit the park compared to other people. You could bring up the medical science that shows how much exercise dogs need to stay healthy, and talk about veterinarians' opinions about the effects of too little exercise on dogs. And you could point to examples from other parks or cities where dog parks have been established, and show statistics about how the number of dog bites has gone down in those places, and how surveys demonstrate that people are happy with the off-leash areas. All of these arguments would be intended to show why the facts demonstrate your solution is the most logical one.

AUTHORITY

LOGIC

EMOTIONS

Why not try all three?

These different kinds of arguments work in different ways, and different people tend to find one kind or another more convincing. What you'll probably want to do is use all three kinds of arguments together. If you're writing a letter or making a speech, you'll want to convince people that you know what you're talking about, get them to feel emotionally involved in the subject, and then convince them your proposal makes logical sense. That's what most people making political arguments do—they combine the different types of argument together into a super-argument.

I see what you did there

Obviously your opponents in any debate will be doing the same thing: they'll be trying to use credibility, emotion, and logic to support their own arguments. And if you want to respond to the points they are making, it helps to be able to really see what kind of rhetoric they're using and how it works.

In fact, one of the main reasons to understand and pay attention to how rhetoric works is not to make better arguments yourself. Most of us will spend more time hearing other people argue about issues than we will making speeches and debating. If we learn how to look at the arguments of others and understand their techniques, we can do a better job making smart decisions.

None of these kinds of arguments is necessarily better or more important than the others. In fact, when you're listening to a political argument, each kind of argument is linked to one of the three main kinds of questions you should ask yourself before deciding what you think.

?? Questions to ask yourself:

Do I trust this person?
- Are they likely to be telling the truth?
- Are they able to do the things they say they will, or do they know about the things they're talking about?
- Is there a good reason for me to think this person knows what they're talking about?

How do I feel about this issue?
- Are my feelings about this making it difficult for me to think clearly about this issue, or to keep an open mind about what people are saying about it?
- Will a particular solution that's proposed make me feel better, or worse, about it?

What does the evidence say?
- Is there a real reason to feel the way I do?
- Does this proposed solution seem likely to work?

CASE STUDY

Rhetoric: "Bumper Sticker Politics" and Barack Obama

Most political campaigns won't make big super-arguments all the time, because they know that most people don't have the time or energy to sit down and listen to them. Instead, for their advertising, politicians and activists will often develop slogans: short sentences or phrases that try to sum up an issue in a memorable way. "Respect for Taxpayers," "The West Wants In," and "I Like Ike" are all examples of slogans that have actually been used. Because these kinds of messages are short enough to fit on a car bumper sticker, people sometimes call the creation and repetition of catchy slogans "bumper sticker politics."

A slogan also helps frame a complicated issue in a certain way. For instance, look at the controversial issue of abortion. People who want abortion to be illegal call themselves "Pro Life," because who's not in favor of life? Meanwhile, the people who want abortion to be legal call themselves "Pro Choice" because, again, almost everyone likes choices. Each side thinks they can win the debate if they can get people to agree that their way of looking at it is what the issue is really about.

When Barack Obama was running for president of the United States in 2008, he used three main slogans that summed up what most of his supporters liked about him.

"Change" was one. At a time when the global economy was in crisis and the United States was at war, a lot of people wanted a change—he simply used the word to tell voters he was the one who would make things different.

"Hope" was another slogan. It reminded people who were feeling helpless that he offered them a reason to think things might change for the better.

Finally, there was "Yes We Can." He used this over and over again in speeches, and his supporters chanted it everywhere. This slogan was a response to people who felt that the system could not be changed. Obama gave a ton of speeches, participated in many debates, and proposed a lot of policies. But if you talk to many of the people who voted for him, those three slogans are probably the things they remember most about his campaign. Together, they summed up what he stood for.

Bumper sticker politics can sometimes be a good thing. It can sum up the important message of a very complicated argument in a way that is easy to understand and remember. But it can also be a problem because short slogans can oversimplify really important issues. And if all that people remember are the slogans, they'll usually have too little information to understand the issues and make a smart decision.

Conflict is good

I have a friend named Misha Glouberman who teaches classes about how to communicate well and resolve conflicts. He first got interested in conflict resolution when he was involved in a political conflict of his own.

Misha lives on a busy street, next door to a restaurant that becomes a nightclub late at night. The loud music used to keep him and his neighbors awake. But no matter how much he complained, he couldn't get them to turn the music down.

Then the restaurant wanted to open a patio out on the street, where they could also play music late into the night. Misha and his neighbors thought they'd never get to sleep again, so they all signed a petition. They found laws that seemed to suggest the patio might not be legal, so they started phoning their local city councilor. Eventually, they convinced the councilor to oppose the restaurant's plan.

Basically, Misha and his neighbors were going to stop the patio. And the restaurant

owners who wanted the patio were going to lose.

"We'd won," Misha wrote in his book *The Chairs Are Where the People Go*. "Then something funny happened."

We'll come back to what that something funny was in a moment. But first, let's chat about political conflicts like Misha's.

Arguments are how we learn to get along

Teachers and parents often tell us to "stop arguing" with our brothers and sisters or classmates. We often think about arguments as bad things—a kind of fight, a conflict. And we mostly try to avoid conflict when we can, because it can make people angry. It's easier and more fun to agree on things.

But in a society, we sometimes need conflict, because it's how we figure out how to get along.

People are different. They have different ideas, different preferences, and different ways of living. And those differences are going to mean they get into arguments about how they do things together, or what things they should even bother doing together. Those arguments can get pretty serious.

This isn't necessarily a bad thing. Conflicts can be a good thing if they can be solved peacefully. That's exactly what a good political system is for: successfully navigating conflicts.

Conflict is so important that we make it part of the process

In order to hear all different opinions on an issue, most countries have built debate right into their process. For example, in most legislatures or parliaments, where elected representatives make political decisions, the parties that lost the election will still have representatives present who oppose the government, arguing with them about issues and voting on every decision.

In Canada, the leader of the second-place party in the election is called the Leader of the Official Opposition. They get to live in a special house owned by the government, with the sole job of arguing with the prime minister, providing different perspectives and options for people to consider. There's a similar job in other countries: in the United States, both houses of congress have a minority leader who opposes the majority party (that's the party that received more than half of the votes in the election).

Truth and justice, not winning and losing

If you watch a lot of courtroom dramas on TV, you'll see lawyers who work for the government trying their best to win a case by proving someone is guilty, and congratulating each other when they do. Or acting sad when they lose. But if you talk to real lawyers in most democratic countries, they will tell you that is not how they are supposed to look at their jobs.

In the court systems of most countries, a person accused of a crime is guaranteed the right to have a lawyer—the defense. They argue against the lawyer who provides evidence from the police—the prosecutor. This is based on the belief that having the two sides present all their evidence is the best way to find the truth.

And that's the point of the process, to find the truth. Not to win, or lose. The lawyers' jobs are to make sure they put all the relevant facts in front of the court and provide the best arguments they can. If they both do that, then the court can make the best decision possible. And if the court makes the best decision, then the lawyers have not "won" or "lost," they've just helped the system produce justice.

Ideally, politics can work the same way. And sometimes it does.

Something better than winning

Let's get back to my friend Misha and the funny thing that happened next.

After Misha thought he had won his argument about the restaurant patio, his city councilor suggested he and his neighbors talk to the restaurant owners to see if they could compromise. At first, Misha thought that it was crazy to ask him to compromise. He'd already won! But he and his neighbors finally agreed to sit down and talk to the restaurant owners.

It turned out the restaurant owners didn't want to have a patio that played loud music late at night; they mainly wanted it for dinnertime business. And the residents didn't care about the dinnertime noise; they only wanted to be able to sleep. The owners of the restaurant were willing to cut off all the loud music late at night—not just on the patio but inside the restaurant, where the noise was already bothering the neighbors—if they could have a patio open at dinnertime. Everyone agreed that this was a great solution.

"So, in fact, this compromise was a better outcome than the victory we had imagined for ourselves," Misha wrote in his book. "And that stayed with me forever. I think it's an incredible lesson. The fact that something can be better than winning in an apparently antagonistic situation like this seems so important."

More voices equals better decisions

What Misha realized was that even in an argument that seemed as though it had to have a winner and a loser, it was possible for everyone to get what they really wanted. But for that to happen, they first had to have the argument, then also realize that compromise and negotiation could be part of resolving that conflict.

There are actually a lot of studies that show this is true in a bunch of different situations. Research shows that the more voices you have around a table making a decision, the better their solution will be. Almost all groups will make a better decision than their smartest, most expert member would come up with on their own. This diversity of opinions, experiences, and perspectives involved will almost always lead to better results—ones that suit the needs of the group, and that address the conflicts that exist within the group.

Getting the crowd involved

Just to consider an example, let's look at the field of urban planning. The job of figuring out how to build and improve cities has been transformed by the idea of the wisdom of crowds. Planners used to think experts could draw up the best solution for a community all by themselves, putting the things a city needed in the places that made the most sense. The experts would make a map and draw in all the parts. Then it would be built like that for people to live in.

In the real world, however, this led to people not liking the places they lived in all that much. It caused a lot of problems. Now planners tend to think that one of the most important parts of their job is collaborating with the people who live and work in an area they're working on. Consultation, public meetings, and sharing information has become just as important as the opinions of the experts.

This has been found to be true not just in city planning but in all kinds of fields that deal day to day with making decisions for a society. In other words, the fields that are involved in politics.

CASE STUDY

The Wisdom of Crowds

An American writer named James Surowiecki wrote a book called *The Wisdom of Crowds* about how groups—even very large groups—usually make better decisions than individual people. In that book, he relates a particularly famous case that demonstrates this idea.

In 1906, a scientist named Francis Galton went to a fair, where there was a contest that asked people to guess the weight of an ox. Eight hundred people entered the contest, writing their guesses down on paper. The winner of the contest was nine pounds off. But when Galton looked at the results, he noticed that the average of all the guesses was only one pound away from the animal's actual weight. The group as a whole was closer than any of the guesses were, even those of cattle experts who were on hand at the fair.

This insight has led to lots of research that backs up the case, as Surowiecki writes, but it shows that the wisdom of crowds depends a lot on having lots of diversity in the crowd—lots of people with different backgrounds—and on the independence of the people in their decision-making.

chapter 6

Conflict can also be bad

Have you ever played soccer? If everyone knows what the rules are, and the game is played fairly by everyone, and everyone participates and tries their hardest, then it can be a lot of fun—no matter what the score winds up being.

But imagine some of the players don't understand the rules. Other players cheat every chance they get...and don't get caught by the referee. Then imagine that a few players who feel they can't keep up just sit down on the field instead of playing, while still other people who are afraid of losing don't try to score or pass or play properly, and instead they just keep kicking the ball out of bounds all the time so no one else can touch it.

That doesn't sound like a fun game of soccer, does it? In fact, it wouldn't be much like a game of soccer at all. Most of the people playing would just wind up feeling frustrated and wouldn't want to play anymore.

Sometimes politics can be a bit like that. And because getting everyone involved in making decisions is so important, this can lead to pretty bad outcomes.

Thinking of your fellow citizens as enemies

People sometimes forget that politics is a process of discussion and trade-offs. We share our ideas and opinions with each other, debate them, and then make some compromises that we can all live with in order to get things done. We can't always get everything we want, and that's okay. That's how almost everything in life works. And that's how the political system is supposed to work.

But sometimes people with certain ideas about how society or the government should run—like political parties or activist groups or businesses—get so caught up in the act of debating that they start to think of politics as a fight. A debate and a fight might seem like the same thing, but there's a small, important difference. In a debate, you exchange different ideas, and try to convince someone of something. In a fight, you try to beat someone. When you convince someone through debate, they willingly join your side. When you beat them, they lose and get hurt or angry. This single difference changes a lot.

When people think of politics as a fight, they get obsessed with winning and losing. Instead of realizing that the reason for the debate in the first place is to decide how to live together, they start thinking of those they disagree with as their enemies. It's as if they are playing a sport or, worse, fighting in a war.

Polarization: When politics drives people apart instead of bringing them together

When people think of those who disagree with them as enemies, it leads to a situation called polarization. This means people's opinions are so far apart that they have a hard time even understanding each other. They start to think people who disagree with them are bad people. They don't trust each other.

You may have heard people talk about partisanship. This means that people from one political party or group see themselves as a team (which they are, in a way) and start to view supporting this team as more important than anything else. They'll oppose good ideas just because they come from a political opponent, or the "other team." Meanwhile, they'll defend terrible behavior only because it's done by "their team."

When things get really polarized, it can lead to something called legislative gridlock. That's when the different parties who are involved in government stop even trying to have an honest debate to get things done and just start blocking each other from accomplishing anything. How? Most government systems have safeguards that stop people from cheating or turning controversial bills into laws too quickly. This can sometimes slow down the process of passing laws, for good reason. But in legislative gridlock, opposing parties use these procedures deliberately just to make sure their opponents don't get anything done. And, predictably, the result is that nothing gets done.

Can you care too much?

To be fair, a lot of these polarization problems happen because people care so much about the things they are arguing about. After all, these issues are important. Decisions about war and peace and jobs and taxes can have a huge impact on the quality of people's lives. So people are passionate. But they start to think that people who feel differently just don't care about these life-and-death issues. Or even worse, that they are kind of evil. That's just one of the problems passion can cause in politics.

Usually, we think of passion as a good thing. When people are really convinced that what they're doing is important, they work very hard. But too much passion can be a bad thing in politics because it

WHERE DID YOU READ THAT?

Today there are a lot of different ways to get information—different books, TV shows, newspapers, the Internet. There are so many places that a lot of the time, people read entirely different kinds of information from each another. This can make it hard for people to agree even about the basic facts in any debate. It's as if some people playing a game thought they were playing soccer, and others thought they were playing basketball, and a few thought they were playing *Minecraft*. That's why honest debate—without polarization—is so important. It helps everyone exchange ideas together and more easily find common ground.

makes us resist compromising. It can lead good people to do bad things—like lying or cheating—because they think they need to do them in order to be able to accomplish the goals they believe in. And, as I mentioned before, it can make them forget that the people they disagree with are also trying their best to make the world a better place.

When we can't imagine that we're all working our hardest to try to get along, it's difficult to make conflict lead to good solutions.

The way our brains work can make good solutions harder

There's a weird quirk in our brains that causes a lot of political problems. We usually think we have used facts to make up our minds—and that we would change our minds if we got evidence to show us something different. But experiments show that we don't always do this.

For instance, fans of opposing sports teams watch a play in which a player falls down. Those rooting for one team will believe the player was knocked down by his opponent and the referee should have called a foul. But fans of the other team will believe the player just fell on his own. Even after they watch a bunch of replays, both sides will continue to believe their own version. They actually see the same play differently because of how much they like one team over the other.

The thing is, everyone experiences this. It's called selective perception, which is a kind of confirmation bias. Confirmation bias simply means this: if we believe something, we tend to look at any new evidence in a way that supports our belief. Even when we see evidence that really should lead us to change our minds, we either refuse to believe it or we dismiss it as unimportant.

Selective perception and confirmation bias are two reasons arguments get so angry and polarized: people in disagreements think their opponents are ignoring facts. And often they are. But it's not just them. It's everyone.

We all suffer from confirmation bias, and we're almost never aware of it in ourselves. We think we have an opinion for a good reason, and when we read things about an issue, we notice and believe and remember the things that back up our opinion. But we ignore things that would make us change our minds. We don't even know we're doing it, but we are.

This is really hard to overcome. But when you know it exists, you can look more closely at the evidence and see how your feelings are changing your reaction to that information. Then you can remember that people who disagree with you usually aren't lying when they say they see the facts differently. They actually *do* see them differently.

Getting the party started

In most of the world, people who want to run for political office organize themselves into groups called political parties. People who make up parties usually agree on some important principles and ways of looking at the world.

But when you think about how dividing into teams can turn politics into a bitter fight instead of a healthy debate, you may start to wonder: Why do we need these political parties at all? Wouldn't it be better if we all just participated in the process as independent citizens? Then we could consider each issue on its merits, and vote for a candidate based on what they propose, rather than blindly following whatever group they belong to.

It's tempting to think so. But there's a good reason why people form political parties. A bunch of good reasons, actually.

It's complicated

Society is very complex. And the job of running it is very complicated. There are millions of conflicts in a country, and arguments about all of them are happening everywhere. People, and groups of people, are always trying to persuade others to see their point of view so they can get public opinion on their side and make the changes they want made.

But there are so many issues that people can't keep track of them all. And most of these issues are only really important to a small group of people. As a society, we need ways to group issues together so that more people can agree to work on them. By working together, people make sure that they focus on their common goals. They can set priorities to decide

how to tackle problems, and determine which things need to be done right away and which should be done later. And they avoid running against each other in elections, which would force people to choose between two candidates who stand for the same ideas.

This is where political parties come in.

Joining a group is natural

Forming groups is a normal part of how we behave as human beings. In schools, online, and everywhere else in our lives, we form clubs with other people that share our interests. There are chess clubs where people can find others to play against, book clubs where people can discuss what they're reading, and online forums where people can talk about their favorite movies. When we're interested in something, we find other people who can talk about it and do it with us.

And when we do that, we get a few benefits, other than making friends. We can organize things like chess games so that we have opponents to play and regular times when we know we can get together for matches. We also learn from each other by sharing our knowledge about the things we're interested in and talking about the differences in our observations, which makes us smarter and better at the things we're doing. It can help us choose things: for example, a book club can choose which book all its members will read next, out of the

hundreds of millions of books available.

Members of political parties get the same kinds of benefits.

Groups in democracy

Political parties in a democracy offer a practical benefit on top of the normal ones that come with being part of a group. Think of an election. If you have a group of people who will not only work together but also vote together, then it is much easier to win a majority of the votes. People who find that they want

government to do a lot of the same kinds of things will get together as a political party so that they can count on each other's votes.

Finally, when almost all of the people who want to run for office form parties with those who mostly agree with them, it offers regular voters a few well-defined options to consider. That makes things easy to keep track of, which makes it manageable to be informed and interested.

CASE STUDY

The Ideological Spectrum

Usually, political parties are formed based on a shared ideology. Ideology is the name we give to a person's political worldview—their point of view on politics. It's the way they tend to see things and think about things, and what they think is most important. That makes people's ideology a natural way to form political parties.

The most common way to talk about ideology is to place it on a range between left wing and right wing. (These names come from where people sat in the legislature after the French Revolution.)

Left-wing ideology is usually summed up as a belief that taking care of the good of the group is the most important job of government. Right-wing ideology usually describes a belief that the freedom and good of the individual is most important.

So left-wing parties will usually favor higher taxes to pay for social programs that help people who are struggling (by giving them money, for example), while right-wing parties will usually favor lower taxes and believe that poor people should work harder to end their struggles. Right-wing parties will often say people have a right to carry guns to protect themselves, while left-wing parties will usually favor banning guns because they think that will protect everyone better.

But it's complicated, like everything in politics, and party positions don't always fit neatly into tidy categories. In many places in the world, for instance, the parties we think of as right wing support limiting individual freedoms for what they think is the greater good: they are in favor of censorship, in favor of banning personal decisions about sexuality and drug use, and believe in giving more power to police to stop and search people without evidence. Meanwhile, parties we think of as left wing support more individual freedom on these issues instead of focusing on the good of the group as a whole.

It's important to note that while most people will describe their beliefs as tending towards the left wing or the right wing, there is a lot of room in between the two extremes.

Here are some terms we frequently apply to describe ideology:

Progressive: Usually a left-wing ideology that says the government should be an active force in trying to change society for the better.

Socialist: A left-wing ideology that believes the government should control the economy for the good of the people, rather than allowing businesses to operate for profit without restrictions. Socialists tend to favor people's well-being over their freedom from government interference.

LEFT WING → RIGHT WING →

Libertarian: A right-wing ideology that says the government has almost no rights to interfere with the individual except to protect them. Libertarians tend to believe that people should be able to do anything they want unless they directly hurt someone else.

Liberal: This word has different meanings in different contexts. Traditionally, it meant someone who believed in capitalism and freedom from government restriction, and it is still often used this way in the phrase "economic liberal." But in North America today, liberal often just means left-wing, although it is thought of as less extreme than socialism.

Conservative: A generally right-wing ideology that says change should happen slowly and the way things are should be preserved. Despite its actual meaning, in North America the term conservative is often used as a catch-all term to mean right-wing.

chapter 8

Avoiding the tyranny of the majority

There used to be a law in Canada, as in other countries, that said only a heterosexual couple—a man and a woman—could get married to each other. A marriage of a man to another man, or of a woman to another woman, was against the law. Many people thought this was unfair, but they couldn't get enough support in public opinion to change the law.

Then in 2003, a court in the province of Ontario ruled that these laws were unconstitutional—that gay and lesbian people had the same right to marry as everyone else. Right away, the law was changed. Thousands of people who weren't allowed to legally marry their partners before had weddings in Ontario. In the year after that, courts in some other parts of Canada made similar decisions. Finally, in 2005, the government of Canada wrote a new law for marriage, recognizing same-sex marriages across the country.

Courts in the United States have been making similar decisions recently. A national U.S. law forbade the government from recognizing same-sex marriages, but the Supreme Court struck that law down as unconstitutional in 2013. Then, in 2015, they also struck down state bans on same-sex marriage, legalizing it across the country.

Why is this significant? Even though elected representatives in government make the laws, sometimes the courts can change the laws. Earlier in the book, I wrote about constitutions, and how they are the law that rules over all laws. Courts have the job of striking down or changing laws that they find violate the principles outlined in the constitution. Even if a majority of people support a law, if it's unconstitutional, the courts will strike it down.

Beyond public opinion

We've already established that public opinion is the most important element in politics, and that in a democracy, the people express their opinion by electing representatives who govern. But there are reasons why we have set up systems—such as courts interpreting the constitution—to restrict the power of elected officials and even public opinion. The idea of a constitution is that it describes the most important principles or values that a country is based on, and sometimes these principles and values have to override the laws passed by politicians.

One of the most important reasons to restrict the power of elected officials is to protect the rights of minorities. In a democracy, when a majority of people—more than half—think a certain way, they can control the elections process. We set up constitutions because we think it's important that the majority of voters do not control the political process in ways that hurt the minority. Especially when it comes to possible violations of human rights. (This is sometimes called "the tyranny of the majority.")

This is what the courts are doing in the case of same-sex marriage, for example—protecting a minority. In the past, courts have used the constitution to protect the rights of religious groups, racial minorities, and people who have unpopular opinions, among others. If someone thinks a law violates their rights, they can go to court to try to get the law struck down or changed.

We call this a "check" on democracy. The courts check to make sure that democracy is working properly, according to the principles the people laid out in the constitution.

But the constitution and the courts are not the only check.

Keeping governments honest

Most governments are set up with different branches that check each other. In the United States, where the whole system is meant to provide "checks and balances" on the power of officials, Congress is made up of two different elected bodies—the House of Representatives and the Senate. Both halves of Congress have to pass every law, then the president has to sign it and enforce it, and finally, courts make sure it is constitutional. All these different groups act as checks on each other's power. Most governments also have people whose job it is to make sure the public gets information and that elected officials are not lying or abusing their power.

These kinds of checks are built right into the system. But there are still other checks on government. Most of them are not as official, even though they are recognized as important parts of our society.

The press

Many countries' constitutions recognize that freedom of the press is an important part of how government operates. There are all kinds of journalists—writing for newspapers, television stations, radio stations, magazines, blogs, websites, and more—who work to tell people about what governments are doing or are considering doing. In democratic countries, they are independent from the government—the government has no control over what the press writes or says. The press acts as an important source of information for the people living in a society, helping them to know what the government is doing, and to decide how to vote or when to get involved.

The public

People affected by the decisions a government makes are also an important check on the power of elected officials. The public constantly watches what's going on to see how it will affect people and the things they care about, and the public will try to influence the government and influence opinion. Businesses will often want to have a big say in laws that affect what they can do, and in the way the society runs in general. Often business owners will hire representatives called lobbyists to try to convince politicians to make decisions that are good for their company. Businesses can also run big advertising campaigns to convince the public to support certain kinds of political decisions.

The activists

People who have a political idea they want to see implemented will often form groups to try to work together to influence the government. Since these people are getting active to change things, we call them activists. Sometimes they have a bunch of ideas they work for over a period of many years—like environmental groups who try to influence all kinds of ecological decisions or taxpayer groups who are always arguing for lower taxes. Sometimes they form groups just to discuss one issue or proposal—to stop a highway from being built, for example, or to change one law they think is unfair.

Businesses and activist groups working to influence decisions are more than just a check on government. They're examples of one of the things this book has been trying to point out all along. For government to function properly, it needs each of us to realize we're a kind of politician. Good government needs more than just professional politicians; it needs citizens who are paying attention, and sometimes getting involved. That's what we'll focus on some more in the next chapter.

Lobbyist: a person paid by a company to try to convince politicians to do what their client wants. A drug manufacturer might pay a lobbyist to persuade politicians to make their drug legal, for instance. Lobbyists are considered a fair part of the process, but there are lots of restrictions in most places on how they can operate. They are usually banned from giving gifts to politicians, and in many countries, their interactions with government officials are closely tracked.

CASE STUDY

Checks and Balances:
Watergate and the Power of the Press

If you hear about any political scandal at all, there's a good chance someone will call it a word ending in "gate." Travelgate, Nannygate, Pastagate—all of these are among the dozens of real political scandals on the Wikipedia page for "List of scandals with -gate suffix." At this point, if you come into school without your math problems done, your teacher might call it "homeworkgate."

This "gate" was first opened way back—forty years ago—with the Watergate scandal. U.S. president Richard Nixon's campaign team had broken into a rival candidate's office at the Watergate Hotel in Washington, D.C. The burglars were arrested by the FBI, but it wasn't until two reporters from the *Washington Post*, Bob Woodward and Carl Bernstein, started reporting on the connections between the break-in and the president that the real scandal emerged. It turned out that the president and his advisers, as well as high-level government agencies like the Justice Department, FBI, and CIA, were all involved in trying to hide the break-in and other "dirty tricks" committed by the Republican Party under Nixon.

When the press brought all this to light, and as Congress was investigating, public opinion about Nixon turned sour, and he was forced to resign. A book was written and a movie was made about the reporters from the *Post*, because without their work, the corruption might never have been known. And we'd need to find another word to put on the end of our scandals.

chapter 9

Knowledge is power

Before you learned how to read, you had to depend on other people to give you information about a lot of things. Your parents or your teachers would tell you facts about the world, or read a book to you so you could understand the story, or tell you how to do things. If you had a question, and they weren't around or they didn't know, you'd get no answer. Or if they told you something that wasn't true, you'd have no way to check that. You were dependent on other people to teach you about things.

But when you learned how to read, suddenly you could find the answers to your questions on your own. Why is the sky blue? How do you make a papier-mâché puppet? What's the story of Jack and the Beanstalk? Once you knew how to read, you had the power to teach yourself these things. And having knowledge is powerful: it is the tool you need to be able to figure out the best way to do something, and it is the tool you need to be able to tell if someone else is doing something wrong.

It's especially powerful for citizens in a political system.

When you don't understand how the system works, or what the important issues are all about, you have to trust other people—politicians or government employees—to tell you what's best. If they're doing things wrong, you won't know. And if you find out they're doing things wrong, you won't be able to do anything to fix it because you won't really understand what the problems are.

But...when you understand how things work, and you pay attention and learn about what people are arguing about, you have the power to be part of making things better.

A more informed community will always mean a better government.

The power of the citizen

Remember active citizenship? How people getting involved can make a real difference in how governments operate? This is an idea that has been around as long as democracy has been talked about and written about: people in democracies acting not just as voters or taxpayers or residents, but as citizens.

Since ancient times, the role of the citizen has been to participate in the government. A citizen is not only allowed to vote, but is also someone who has a lot of rights and responsibilities to the society he or she lives in. A citizen participates in debates, pays taxes, serves on juries, and sometimes serves in the military. In most definitions of citizenship, a key element is that a citizen is an active participant in how society runs and how the government functions.

Think of the classroom at school. Your textbooks give you a lot of good information. But those books are only a part of learning and succeeding. You also need to listen to your teacher, ask questions during class, do homework and activity assignments that let you put what you're learning to good use, participate in group work...and, of course, get along with your fellow students and make friends. By being actively involved at school, you learn and experience so much more than you would by just reading the textbook.

It's the same way in politics. It isn't just happening around you. You are a part of it, and it works better if you actively participate.

As the scholar Derek Benjamin Heater put it in his book *A Brief History of Citizenship*, a society depends on the participation of its citizens. But the citizens "need the skills appropriate for this civic participation." What are those skills, and how do we make sure we have them and use them?

It all starts with knowing things

The good news is that the biggest duty of a citizen is simply to know what's going on. Because public opinion is so important to politics, being able to form well-considered opinions is the most important thing a citizen can do. Knowledge gives you options. Citizens with knowledge have the power to

- ensure politicians are getting good **results**, and spot incompetence or corruption.

- **participate** in debates about important questions, and stop politicians from using people's ignorance for their own benefit.

- **recognize** when the arguments or slogans people are using are wrongheaded, divisive, or designed to fool you.

- draw good **conclusions** about which policies make the most sense and why.

With everything you read, every discussion you have, you're developing the skills of citizenship. In fact, just by learning about things, you're becoming a powerful citizen. Once you're informed, you have the power to form valuable opinions and influence others. And as you know by now, that's the key thing that makes politics work.

MORE SOURCES OF KNOWLEDGE

The good news is that we live in an information supermarket. This is a time when there are lots and lots of ways to learn about politics and issues—more ways than ever before:

- Talking with friends and family is the most basic way to share information and ideas about the things that are happening.

- The news—on TV and radio, in newspapers and magazines, and online—always offers lots of information about political issues and government that comes from professional reporters who study politics as a full-time job.

- Books! You're reading one now, and of course, it's just a start. There are detailed books about any specific political topic you might want to read about in your library or bookstore.

- Websites and blogs offering opinion and analysis provide different points of view from all kinds of people. Websites run by experts like historians, economists, and scientists can teach you a whole lot about specific topics that people may be debating. It's also useful to do research to check out who created the website, to see their point of view. Websites run by political parties or lobbyists, for example, will usually have a certain biased point of view.

- Governments have their own websites, and in many or most places, they post news and information about decisions, meeting schedules, government services, taxes, and all kinds of other topics.

- Social media—like Twitter, Facebook, and YouTube—are great for both information sharing and discussion of issues.

Power of the people

I began this book telling you that you are a politician. That might have seemed like a crazy idea at the time. But now that we've reached the end, I hope you understand what I meant: that you, and all of us, have an important job to play in the political system. As residents and citizens.

Politics depends on what we think and do to function properly. The professional politicians we elect to run our government care about what we think, and they listen to us. And if we ever get the impression that they aren't listening to us, there are ways that we can make them.

When we involve ourselves in politics as informed community members, then we are a part of political decision-making. But if we don't pay attention, and don't actively involve ourselves as residents and citizens, then other people will make decisions for us, decisions we may not like. And they'll only be able to do that because we have let them. All by ignoring politics.

As the ancient philosopher Plato wrote, "One of the penalties of refusing to participate in politics is that you end up being governed by your inferiors."

If you want to participate, you've now learned how. By understanding a bit about how the whole system works. (You've begun understanding that just by reading this book.) By staying informed about what's going on and sharing your understanding of it with those around you—even arguing with them sometimes. Maybe, sometimes, by letting your elected officials and those around you know what you want to change, and what you want to stay the same. And, of course, when you're old enough, you can participate by voting and getting involved with political parties or activist organizations.

But you don't need to wait for that to help shape our politics. You can begin right now. Simply by paying attention and forming intelligent opinions.

It all starts by realizing that politics is not something that happens among powerful people, something that's separate from you. It's something you participate in. Something that gives you power to shape the society you live in.

As a wise superhero once said, "With great power comes great responsibility."

Now you know that you have political power. How you use it is up to you.

glossary

Absolute monarchy: A form of government in which an unelected monarch holds absolute power over a country's decision-making.

Active citizenship: An approach to politics and society that says each person is responsible for trying to make the system work better by learning about it and participating in it.

Anarchy: A system in which there is no government at all and people informally reach arrangements to govern themselves.

Autocracy: A form of government in which power is in the hands of a single person. A dictatorship is an example of an autocratic system.

Collaborating: Working together to achieve a goal.

Confirmation bias: A tendency to look for information that supports the beliefs we already hold, or interpret new information in a way that supports those beliefs. Selective perception is a form of confirmation bias.

Conflict: A disagreement or fight, usually caused because two or more people or groups of people want different things.

Constitution: A law overriding all others that expresses a country's fundamental values and principles and lays out the rules for how the whole government and political system will work.

Constitutional monarchy: A form of government in which decisions are made by a democratically elected legislature, while a monarch acts as a check to ensure that all laws are constitutional, and also serves as a symbolic leader.

Consultation: The process of seeking advice or opinions on a topic before making a decision. In urban planning and politics, it usually refers to attempts to hear the opinions and ideas of the people in a community who will be affected by the decision.

Coup: A takeover of the government by force, usually by a group of people from within the government. For example, a military coup occurs when the armed forces of a government overthrow the rulers. Also often called a coup d'état, which is French for "blow of the state."

Democracy: A system in which all people of voting age get to vote on decisions, and often vote to appoint an individual or a group of people who will have the power to make most decisions.

Dictatorship: A system of government in which power is in the hands of one person. A dictatorship is a form of autocracy.

Direct democracy: A system in which every member of a group gets to vote on every decision. Usually not a practical system for large governments (although a few cities in the world do use it for parts of their governing).

Diversity: An array of different things existing together.

Filibuster: A procedure, usually used in a legislature, that tries to delay voting on a law or other measure through the use of speeches. Sometimes these speeches can last hours or even days, without breaks. The intention is usually to reach a time limit that requires the legislature to stop its session, so that the vote in question will never happen.

Ideology: A political worldview based on some fundamental principles that shape a person's opinions on most subjects. People who identify themselves with an ideological group will use those beliefs to guide their political decisions.

Legislative gridlock: A situation in which no laws can be passed in a legislature because the various parties in it find ways to block each other's progress.

Legislature: The assembly where elected officials meet to debate and make laws. In the United States, both houses of Congress—the House of Representatives and the Senate—are legislatures. In many countries, the legislature is called a parliament. Sometimes a legislature will have other names, such as "assembly," "council," or "diet."

Oligarchy: A form of government in which power is in the hands of a very few people.

Partisanship: A form of prejudice in favor of the members and policies of a political party.

Polarization: In politics, the concentration of opinion at two opposing extreme ends of a spectrum. In normal circumstances, opinions will present a range across a spectrum.

When things become polarized, people overwhelmingly cluster at the far ends of the spectrum, unable to agree with each other on much of anything.

Policy: A decision that the government (or other group) makes about something it will do or that people will have to do. A new tax is a policy. Building bridges comes from a policy. Going to war is a policy.

Process: In politics, the way a decision is made. Who gets to vote? Whose opinions are heard about the decision before it is made? Who gets the final say? The answers to these questions outline the process.

Representative democracy: A form of democracy in which citizens elect representatives to govern on their behalf. This differs from direct democracy, where every citizen votes on every law or governing decision.

Rhetoric: The art of persuading people using writing or speech, and the study of the techniques used to do that.

Selective perception: A tendency to not notice or to quickly forget evidence that goes against our own beliefs or feelings. This is a kind of confirmation bias.

Threat: Any person, group of people, animal, force of nature (like a tidal wave, fire, or disease) that might hurt someone. Threats can hurt people by physically attacking them, or by wrecking or taking away their belongings or their sources of food.

sources

"7 Teen Girls Who are Changing the World," *Buzzfeed*, March 3, 2014. Online.

"Beyond Malala: Six Teenagers Changing The World," *The Guardian*, October 18, 2013. Online.

Boston Tea Party Historical Society. "What Was the Boston Tea Party?" Online.

Clinton, Chelsea. "The *Time* 100: Malala Yousafzai," April 18, 2013, *Time*. Online.

Cohen, David. "The Curious Case of Zhan Haite," *The Diplomat*, December 19, 2012. Online.

"History: Egyptians," BBC News. Online.

Galton, Francis. "Vox Populi (The Wisdom of Crowds)," *Nature*, Vol. 75, 1949. Full article accessed through *All About Psychology*. Online.

Glouberman, Misha. *The Chairs Are Where the People Go: How to Live, Work, and Play in the City*. New York: Faber and Faber, 2011.

"Guangdong to Loosen School Entry Restrictions for Migrants, but Some Say It's Not Enough," *The Nanfang*, December 31, 2012. Online

Hastorf, Albert H. and Cantril, Hadley, "They Saw a Game; A Case Study," *The Journal of Abnormal and Social Psychology*, Vol 49 (1), Jan 1954. Accessed at American Psychological Association PsycNET. Online.

Heater, Derek Bemjamin, *A Brief History of Citizenship*. Oxford University Press, 2004.

Kaphle, Anup. "Timeline: Egypt's Rocky Revolution," *The Washington Post*, August 19, 2013.

Martin, Douglas. "Jane Jacobs, Urban Activist, Is Dead at 89," *New York Times*, April 25, 2006.

Mays, Jeff. "Georgia Teen Mary-Pat Hector Urges Young People to 'Think Twice' Before Picking Up a Gun," NewsOne, February 1, 2014. Online.

National Action Network. "Mary-Pat Hector— National Youth Director." Online.

Project for Public Spaces. "Jane Jacobs." Online.

Sengeh, David. "DIY Africa: Empowering a New Sierra Leone," CNN, November 14, 2012. Online.

Surowiecki, James. *The Wisdom of Crowds: Why the Many Are Smarter Than the Few and How Collective Wisdom Shapes Business, Economies, Societies, and Nations*. New York, Little, Brown. 2004.

acknowledgments

I owe a great debt of gratitude to John Crossingham, my editor at OwlKids Books, for coming to me with the idea for a kids' book about politics that wouldn't be just another how-a-bill-becomes-a-law text, and for his patience and wisdom at every stage of creating it. Also to everyone at OwlKids, especially the Karens (Li and Boersma) for their generosity, help, and guidance. And, of course, many thanks to Julie McLaughlin for illustrations that capture the spirit of the thing, and designer Barb Kelly for making it all come alive on the page.

I also must thank my editors and colleagues at the *Toronto Star*, *Spacing* magazine, Newstalk 1010, and the dearly departed *Grid* and *Eye Weekly*, for giving me the opportunity to observe politics in action over a long period of years, and to think, talk, and write about it at length.

And to those in Toronto—friends, subjects, and sometimes opponents—who've taught me about politics over the years, by showing me their lives and work as an example, including especially friends Angela Valentini and Dave Meslin, mayors David Miller and Rob Ford, and all the members of Toronto city council and the other legislative bodies I've written about over the years. My understanding of how it all works would be far more limited if I had not had the chance to see them all in action. Thanks.

And finally thanks to my family for giving me all the practical lessons I need in the art of the possible—and the highly improbable—and making it all seem worthwhile: my parents, Donna and Edward; my siblings Sean, Andrew, and Tara; and my children, Colum, Irene, and Mary. And of course Rebecca, whose patience, love, and level-headed support was essential to making this book itself possible.

index